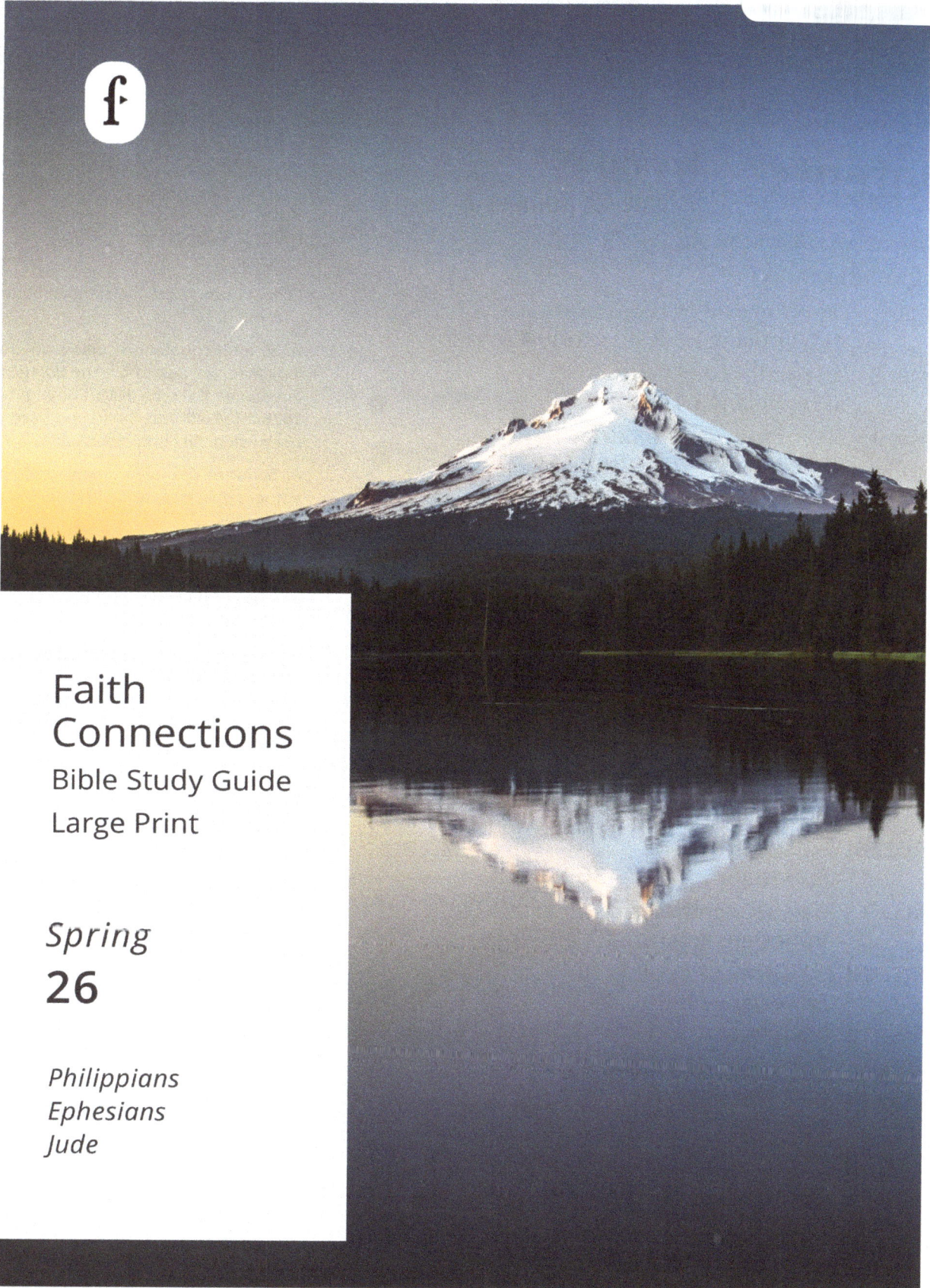

Faith Connections

Bible Study Guide

Large Print

Spring
26

Philippians
Ephesians
Jude

Bible Study Guide

Contents

Spring 2026
Volume 49, Number 3

Mike L. Wonch
Editor

Cover Photo: © ESB Professional/Shutterstock. com

All scripture quotations, unless otherwise indicated, are taken from the *Holy Bible, New International Version* (NIV). Copyright © 1973, 1978, 1984, 2011 by Biblica Inc. Used by permission. All rights reserved.

All Scripture quotations marked † are the author's own translation from the original languages.

We believe in the full inspiration of the Scripture and encourage the comparison and use of several translations as part of the discipline of Bible study.

Bible Study Guide is published quarterly by The Foundry Publishing®, P.O. Box 419527, Kansas City, MO 64141. Copyright © 2026 by The Foundry Publishing®. Canadian GST No. R129017471.

Adult Bible Study Guide is one of several Faith Connections companion products, a themed suite of resources designed to help adults discover what it means to be holy people in today's world. To order, call 1-800-877-0700.

Perspectives

I Want to Know!

The National Enquirer is a tabloid magazine that centers on Hollywood gossip, crime news, and other so-called investigative reporting. This magazine touts that it provides stories that "inquiring minds want to know." Stories include secrets of celebrity couples, crime conspiracy theories, and uncovering clues that might indicate Elvis is still alive—with a circulation of tens of thousands, apparently these are stories that some people want to know. But what's worth knowing?

Paul writes in Philippians 3:10, "I want to know Christ." Paul had encountered the risen Christ on the Damascus Road, and it changed his life. From that point forward, his life was spent preaching the gospel, establishing churches, and pursuing a deeper relationship with Christ. Before meeting Christ, Paul had impressive Jewish credentials. He had been a Hebrew of Hebrews—circumcised on the eighth day, a member of the tribe of Benjamin, and a Pharisee (Philippians 3:5-6). Yet, after meeting the Savior, his focus changed. Rather than building his religious resume, he sought to "know Christ and the power of his resurrection."

Paul considered "everything a loss because of the surpassing worth of *knowing* Christ Jesus my Lord, for whose sake I have lost all things. I consider them garbage, that I may gain Christ" (Philippians 3:8, emphasis added). For Paul, "gaining Christ goes hand in glove with *knowing* Christ."[1] New Testament scholar Dean Flemming points out, "On one hand, Paul has already gained Christ through coming to know him in his conversion. On the other, he is still on a journey, which will only be completed when he gains Christ in a full and final sense on the last day."[2]

Knowing Christ is not about just knowing how He lived or what He taught, although those things are important. Knowing means being in relationship with Him—dedicating our lives to Him. It means identifying with Christ—sharing in His sufferings (see 1 Peter 4:13). That is, "Knowing Christ intensely involves a profound identification with the Christ who suffered—a sharing of his very life and experience."[3]

During your study of Philippians, Ephesians, and Jude, consider what it means to really know Christ. As you do, I pray "the peace of God, which transcends all understanding, will guard your hearts and your minds in Christ Jesus" (Philippians 4:6-7).

May God bless you as you study His Word this quarter!

1. *NBBC: Philippians* (Kansas City: Beacon Hill Press of Kansas City, 2009), 168.
2. Ibid, 168.
3. Ibid, 175.

MIKE WONCH
Editor

March

1

PARTNERSHIP IN THE GOSPEL

Our partnership with other believers in ministry is vital to the life of the church.

THE WORD

PHILIPPIANS 1:3-8

KEY VERSES

I thank my God every time I remember you. **⁴In all my prayers for all of you, I always pray with joy ⁵because of your partnership in the gospel from the first day until now, ⁶being confident of this, that he who began a good work in you will carry it on to completion until the day of Christ Jesus.**

⁷It is right for me to feel this way about all of you, since I have you in my heart and, whether I am in chains or defending and confirming the gospel, all of you share in God's grace with me. ⁸God can testify how I long for all of you with the affection of Christ Jesus.

PHILIPPIANS 4:14-19

¹⁴Yet it was good of you to share in my troubles. ¹⁵Moreover, as you Philippians know, in the early days of your acquaintance with the gospel, when I set out from Macedonia, not one church shared with me in the matter of giving and receiving, except you only; ¹⁶for even when I was in Thessalonica, you sent me aid more than once when I was in need. ¹⁷Not that I desire your gifts; what I desire is that more be credited to your account. ¹⁸I have received full payment and have more than enough. I am amply supplied, now that I have received from Epaphroditus the gifts you sent. They are a fragrant offering, an acceptable sacrifice, pleasing to God. ¹⁹And my God will meet all your needs according to the riches of his glory in Christ Jesus.

ENGAGE THE WORD

Paul writes this letter while he is in prison (more appropriately, house arrest) in Rome (around AD 60-64). He is awaiting trial, and yet even in the midst of what most of us would consider to be a very non-desirable situation, Paul writes what is arguably one of his most personal letters to the Christians at Philippi.

PAUL'S PRAYERS OF THANKSGIVING

Philippians 1:3

Paul began with a declarative statement in which he reminded them that they are often on his mind, and with every memory he has of them, it is an opportunity to thank God for their ongoing partnership with him in the spreading of the gospel. Paul conveys an intensity of his feelings of love and affection for these people, a reflection of the same intensity he demonstrates in his devotion to God. No doubt Paul had many such important relationships in his life (his closing expression of thanks in Romans 16 is one such example). But he makes it clear that his thanksgiving here is not just because of who the Philippians were, but also because of their partnership in the gospel.

JOYFUL ABANDON

Philippians 1:4-5

Paul's prayers are not seen as drudgery or as an obligation. Rather, he prays with a joyful abandon for the Philippians. His joy is expressed because when he prays, he knows the issues they are facing. He understands their needs, and as such, his prayers are more specific, more focused, and convey greater urgency and passion as he knows that only God can meet their needs. But for Paul, this is not a one-way expression of joy in prayer. Rather, Paul is convinced that the Christians in Philippi are praying in the same vein for him. This is part of their ongoing partnership.

One of the most important elements of this passage in Philippians 1 is Paul's claim that he has every reason to express his joy because of their ministry.

Check out "Getting the Most Out of Your Prayer Time" on page 63.

PARTNERSHIP IN GIVING

It is something to be celebrated, to be encouraged, and to recognize it as an extension of Paul's own ministry when he was among them. This is more than simply showing up for Sunday services or giving in the offering. Rather, it is embodying the two greatest commandments: to love God and to love neighbor, no matter what (Matthew 22:36-40).

JOY DEFINES WHO WE ARE

Philippians 1:6-8

The joy that Paul expresses is more than just a mood or a fleeting feeling. Neither is it based on the faithfulness of the Philippians in their continuance of ministry in Paul's absence. Rather, it is a joy that is based on the faithfulness of God who will carry this ministry "on to completion until the day of Christ Jesus" (v. 6). Paul knows that God will ensure His work is done, and yet invites Paul and the church at Philippi to join Him in His ongoing ministry. This assurance is what enables Paul to have joy even while sitting in prison.

This type of joy is what Paul desired for the Philippians (and thus for us). It is a joy that transcends our current situation. Note that it doesn't change the situation, but having an attitude of joy impacts the way we pray for and with others. It alters the way we view things, seeing them as God sees them, and believing that He is bringing all things to completion for His good. It is the recognition that because we are invited to "share in God's grace" we don't walk this journey alone, but we walk it with God and with other fellow believers in ministry.

Philippians 4:14-17

One of the most amazing things that Paul notes in his appreciation for the church at Philippi is their giving after he left them. On his missionary journey, Paul had planted the church there in Philippi, and after a short period of time, he felt called to leave there and

Think About It

An examination of Paul's life reveals that in almost every city in which he found himself, he sought to find like-minded believers to share with him in the gospel delivery. Even with all his gifts (he was an incredibly learned man, one who carried both Roman and Jewish citizenry, articulate), he recognized the importance of giving others the opportunity to partner together for the sake of the gospel. As he reminded both the church in Rome and Corinth, none of us operate alone in this endeavor, for we are all part of the body of Christ.

go to Thessalonica. It is an amazing thing, Paul notes, that even as a new church plant, they took it upon themselves to support Paul's work in Thessalonica. We don't know just how long Paul was in Thessalonica, but apparently it was long enough that Paul, even using his trade of being a tentmaker, was in financial need. The Philippians truly wanted to ensure that the good news they had received was given to others as well, and one of the ways they did this was to ensure Paul's need was addressed.

GIVING AS AN ACT OF WORSHIP
Philippians 4:18-19

The simple giving of resources to assist Paul is more than a human-to-human interaction. Paul makes it clear that their giving is an act of worship. In writing to the church, Paul makes it clear that their investment in him is really a spiritual investment in the gospel and they will receive full credit from God for their generous nature. Their gift, Paul explains, is not simply to provide funding for his work, but is a "fragrant offering" to God, one which God finds very acceptable. Because of their willingness, at great personal cost, to give to supply Paul's needs (and as their act of worship), God in return will ensure their needs are met. After all, He is the giver of all good things.

REFLECT What are the ways that you might provide opportunities for others to join you in the work of the gospel, so that both you and they might offer a fragrant gift of worship to God?

JIM HAMPTON is a professor, speaker, and writer. He is married to Carolyn and they have two adult children.

IN CHAINS FOR CHRIST

Every obstacle can be an occasion for advancing the gospel.

THE WORD

PHILIPPIANS 1:12-26

Now I want you to know, brothers and sisters, that what has happened to me has actually served to advance the gospel. ¹³As a result, it has become clear throughout the whole palace guard and to everyone else that I am in chains for Christ. ¹⁴And because of my chains, most of the brothers and sisters have become confident in the Lord and dare all the more to proclaim the gospel without fear.

¹⁵It is true that some preach Christ out of envy and rivalry, but others out of goodwill. ¹⁶The latter do so out of love, knowing that I am put here for the defense of the gospel. ¹⁷The former preach Christ out of selfish ambition, not sincerely, supposing that they can stir up trouble for me while I am in chains. ¹⁸But what does it matter? The important thing is that in every way, whether from false motives or true, Christ is preached. And because of this I rejoice.

Yes, and I will continue to rejoice, ¹⁹for I know that through your prayers and God's provision of the Spirit of Jesus Christ what has happened to me will turn out for my deliverance. ²⁰I eagerly expect and hope that I will in no way be ashamed, but will have sufficient courage so that now as always Christ will be exalted in my body, whether by life or by death. **²¹For to me, to live is Christ and to die is gain.** ²²If I am to go on living in the body, this will mean fruitful labor for me. Yet what shall I choose? I do not know! ²³I am torn between the two: I desire to depart and be with Christ, which is better by far; ²⁴but it is more necessary for you that I remain in the body. ²⁵Convinced of this, I know that I will remain, and I will continue with all of you for your progress and joy in the faith, ²⁶so that through my being with you again your boasting in Christ Jesus will abound on account of me.

KEY VERSE

Unit 1: Philippians

ENGAGE THE WORD

Throughout the book of Philippians Paul models a Christ-centered perspective. His entire focus is on what it means to live a life so focused on Jesus that everything else is a secondary matter. Paul recognized that his joy, even while imprisoned, came only because of his dependence on Christ.

BAD NEWS LEADS TO GOOD NEWS

Philippians 1:12-14

Despite being in prison, Paul again makes clear that he does not view this as the end of his ministry. Because his focus is on Christ and the propagation of the gospel message, Paul's sole focus is on how his experience has enabled that message to be spread far and wide. He names two specific ways this has happened.

First, because of the way he has modeled Christ it has become apparent to all that he is not in prison for committing any sort of crime, but because he is a follower of Jesus Christ. That gave him the opening he needed to talk with others about why he was imprisoned. Because of his location (the Praetorium of Herod) and amount of time he spent in prison (two years in Caesarea and one year under house arrest in Rome), Paul has been able to share with and impact people from a wide stratum of Roman life and culture. Paul's imprisonment has allowed his message to be heard by a wide variety of soldiers, as they worked in teams to guard him in 4-hour shifts. It seems apparent that their curiosity about Paul and his reason for imprisonment would have allowed ample opportunities to talk with him about why he was there and what he believed. Then, these soldiers would have talked to others about this most curious prisoner. Paul was basically planting the seeds of the gospel in the highest levels of the Roman Empire!

Secondly, Paul states that his imprisonment has emboldened other Christians to "proclaim the gospel without fear" (v. 14). It would have been easy for

FAITHFUL IN LIFE AND DEATH

the other Christians to believe that, since Paul was imprisoned for spreading the word about Christ, perhaps they were better off remaining silent for fear of themselves being locked up. Instead, Paul is overjoyed to see that his imprisonment and his resultant ability to continue the spread of the gospel has actually given others the confidence, even courage, that they too should spread this life-giving message to others, regardless of the consequences. Hearing this brings Paul encouragement and joy.

MOTIVES MATTER
Philippians 1:15-18a

But this joy is tempered. Even though Paul is encouraged by their willingness to boldly proclaim the gospel message, here he adopts the tone of a parent, reminding them that the reason for their proclamation is just as important as their message. He states that while some are preaching out of love and good will, others are driven by petty jealousies, selfish ambition, or envy of their brothers and sisters in Christ. Most likely, this was a group, who for unknown reasons, opposed Paul out of personal animosity and rivalry. Yet, note that Paul still rejoices because, regardless of the motive, Christ is being preached. That has been and continues to be his desire.

Philippians 1:18b-26

Paul's declaration seems foreign to our ears: "For to me, to live is Christ and to die is gain" (v. 21). No one, including Paul, wants to die. But Paul wanted the church at Philippi, those who have been so good to him, to know that despite his great love for them, his love for Christ supersedes that, and their love for Paul should also be surpassed by their love for Christ. Paul knows that his end is near, and while he does not look forward to it, neither does he shrink from it. He knows that whether he is physically released from prison, or simply released from his body, it is the way he

Think About It

Paul's declaration that "to live is Christ and to die is gain" is difficult but necessary for all believers to wrestle with. How do we get to the point that we embrace what is happening and see it as an opportunity to glorify Christ, rather than resisting it because our own desires take precedent? For Paul, even death was ultimately subjugated to the lordship of Christ.

has faithfully lived his life and the message he has so passionately proclaimed that will honor and magnify Christ.

What an intriguing perspective Paul offers! He says he is "torn between the two" (release from prison, or being executed to be with Jesus), indicating he is unsure which is the better option. For him, living is Christ. Everything that Paul has done and will continue to do is built on his trust and dependence on Christ, but more so on the inspiration, direction, meaning, and purpose that Christ offers. Death, and being with Christ, will only amplify that relationship. What Paul does know is that either choice will be an opportunity for the gospel to be furthered.

Paul's perspective on his current circumstances and whether he faces life or death is not a flippant optimism based on a naïve pie-in-the-sky hope that everything will work out. He is not happy that he is imprisoned, but neither does he view it as the end. The Christian does not live with some unutterable longing to escape, to evade life, or to run from it. Rather, Paul holds a view of life and death based upon his relationship with Jesus Christ. In sharing his own reflections on this issue, he is offering the Philippians (and us) a model for how they in turn can also remain faithful even when facing adverse circumstances.

REFLECT Think about what it takes for you to give everything to Christ, including those incredibly difficult circumstances in which you find yourself now and possibly in the future.

JIM HAMPTON

15

STANDING FIRM IN CHRIST

Jesus provides our example of how to remain steady in our faith and the power to do so.

THE WORD

PHILIPPIANS 1:27-30

KEY VERSES

Whatever happens, conduct yourselves in a manner worthy of the gospel of Christ. Then, whether I come and see you or only hear about you in my absence, I will know that you stand firm in the one Spirit, striving together as one for the faith of the gospel 28without being frightened in any way by those who oppose you. This is a sign to them that they will be destroyed, but that you will be saved—and that by God. 29For it has been granted to you on behalf of Christ not only to believe in him, but also to suffer for him, 30since you are going through the same struggle you saw I had, and now hear that I still have.

PHILIPPIANS 2:1-11

1Therefore if you have any encouragement from being united with Christ, if any comfort from his love, if any common sharing in the Spirit, if any tenderness and compassion, 2then make my joy complete by being like-minded, having the same love, being one in spirit and of one mind. 3Do nothing out of selfish ambition or vain conceit. Rather, in humility value others above yourselves, 4not looking to your own interests but each of you to the interests of the others.

5In your relationships with one another, have the same mindset as Christ Jesus: 6Who, being in very nature God, did not consider equality with God something to be used to his own advantage; 7rather, he made himself nothing by taking the very nature of a servant, being made in human likeness. 8And being found in appearance as a man, he humbled himself by becoming obedient to death—even death on a cross!

9Therefore God exalted him to the highest place and gave him the name that is above every name, [10]that at the name of Jesus every knee should bow, in heaven and on earth and under the earth, [11]and every tongue acknowledge that Jesus Christ is Lord, to the glory of God the Father.

ENGAGE THE WORD

HEAVENLY CITIZENSHIP

Philippians 1:27-28

The Philippians are urged to conduct themselves in a "manner worthy of the gospel of Christ." This has overtones of citizenship. Paul reminds them that, as Roman citizens, they know what it means to be a good citizen, both the privileges and the responsibilities. The same, he says, is true of living in the kingdom of God. Live like you know Jesus is your king and your savior. Don't simply add Jesus to your life. Make your life about Jesus.

Paul reminds the Philippians that as Christians they are in a battle and that a united front is the best strategy for victory. It is only in unity that they will be able to withstand the attacks they are facing (v. 28). It takes courage to face attacks, and courage is always in more supply in the community than in the individual. Only as the Philippian Christians struggle together, cooperating fully, can they ensure the real gospel message is faithfully proclaimed.

The focus here is not on eternity but on the current reality they are facing. Paul says that these adversaries see the Philippians fighting for the truth as evidence they will be persecuted and ultimately put to death. But he knows that this struggle collectively for the truth will ensure that even when they endure persecution or suffering, they are saved.

SUFFERING SHOULD BE EXPECTED

Philippians 1:29-30

God has granted the Philippians not just the privilege of belief in Him, but also the privilege of suffering for Him. Paul makes it clear that this suffering is not something to be avoided, but is an act of grace; in our suffering, we learn what we actually believe about

THE ULTIMATE MODEL FOR SERVING OTHERS

God. We also recognize that because Jesus himself suffered, He not only understands our suffering on His behalf, but He walks with us through it, enabling us to identify with Jesus. Paul emphasizes that both he and the Philippians are dealing with suffering for the same reason—namely their determination to preach the gospel and make sure it continues to flourish.

INTERNAL DIVISION AND OUTWARD BEHAVIOR

Philippians 2:1-4

In the preceding verses, Paul recognizes the church at Philippi is in danger, both from outside and inside forces. It is to this latter issue that he now turns his attention.

If the Philippians actually believe what Paul has written to this point, then the logical outcome is that they will seek to model their lives after the risen Lord. To make this point, Paul makes a series of "if...then" statements. These are intended to remind the church that this should be the natural outflow of being "in Christ." But Paul also recognizes that one can experience these things in Christ, but not embody them in our relationship with others. Thus, the "then" part of the statement—if you've experienced all this, then now embody it in your interactions with others. He proceeds to describe the specific ways this should occur—doing nothing out of selfishness, embracing humility, and seeking the best in others.

Philippians 2:5-11

To ensure the Philippians understand what this type of Christlike humility really looks like, he turns to what is known as the "Kenosis" passage, or the Christ-hymn, of verses 5-11. Here, Paul uses material already well known in the church that presents Jesus as the model of what self-giving, obedient, sacrificial humility looks like.

Christ died on our behalf without thought of how it would benefit Him. Similarly, we are called to sacrifi-

Unit 1: Philippians

Think About It

Throughout history Christians have suffered for their stand for God, which has often resulted in loss—property, rights, and even their lives. This is suffering "because of" or "for" Christ. But there's another way to interpret verse 29, namely that we suffer "on behalf of" Christ. This is not to mitigate in any way the sacrificial death of Christ, but to understand that Christ asks people to take His suffering upon themselves in order that others might be saved. Paul was willing to do this for the Philippians. What could Christ possibly ask you to suffer in His stead for the sake of the other?

cially give on behalf of the other, to live with an eye toward ensuring the needs of those around us are met, with no idea toward reward or quid-pro-quo. We do it because, as Paul reminds us, it is the "mindset of Jesus Christ."

Why does Paul point to this hymn as the preeminent example of how to live in Christlike humility? It seems a bit like answering a simple question with a weighty answer. But for Paul, all the issues the church faces are ultimately theological in nature. So, in answer to the question how we live in humility and self-giving, the ultimate example of that humility and sacrificial nature is given. Only the God who gave up heaven to come to earth, who in humility adopted human flesh, and willingly went to the cross knowing the end result, could serve both as the model for what Christlike humility is, and as the one who empowers us to live so.

This same Jesus who exhibited this humility and servanthood is the one to whom we are called to offer our praise and worship. He is the only one that all of creation will ultimately bow to, the one whose name surpasses all others. And according to Paul, it is this Jesus who enables us to move beyond pettiness and jealousy, and instead seek out the path of humility, service, and obedience.

REFLECT Why is humility an important part of exhibiting a Christlike character in our lives?

JIM HAMPTON

I WANT TO KNOW CHRIST

*As believers, we must press forward,
desiring to know the fullness of Christ in our lives.*

THE WORD

**PHILIPPIANS
3:7-21**

But whatever were gains to me I now consider loss for the sake of Christ. [8]What is more, I consider everything a loss because of the surpassing worth of knowing Christ Jesus my Lord, for whose sake I have lost all things. I consider them garbage, that I may gain Christ [9]and be found in him, not having a righteousness of my own that comes from the law, but that which is through faith in Christ—the righteousness that comes from God on the basis of faith. [10]I want to know Christ—yes, to know the power of his resurrection and participation in his sufferings, becoming like him in his death, [11]and so, somehow, attaining to the resurrection from the dead.

[12]Not that I have already obtained all this, or have already arrived at my goal, but I press on to take hold of that for which Christ Jesus took hold of me. **[13]Brothers and sisters, I do not consider myself yet to have taken hold of it. But one thing I do: Forgetting what is behind and straining toward what is ahead, [14]I press on toward the goal to win the prize for which God has called me heavenward in Christ Jesus.**

KEY VERSES

[15]All of us, then, who are mature should take such a view of things. And if on some point you think differently, that too God will make clear to you. [16]Only let us live up to what we have already attained.

[17]Join together in following my example, brothers and sisters, and just as you have us as a model, keep your eyes on those who live as we do. [18]For, as I have often told you before and now tell you again even with tears, many live as enemies of the cross of Christ. [19]Their

Unit 1: Philippians

destiny is destruction, their god is their stomach, and their glory is in their shame. Their mind is set on earthly things. ²⁰But our citizenship is in heaven. And we eagerly await a Savior from there, the Lord Jesus Christ, ²¹who, by the power that enables him to bring everything under his control, will transform our lowly bodies so that they will be like his glorious body.

ENGAGE THE WORD

THE ULTIMATE GOAL IS KNOWING CHRIST

Philippians 3:7-11

In the previous verses, Paul has outlined all the assets, the privileges, that he had. And now he turns that upside down, basically declaring them as worthless. Those benefits, he declares, have absolutely no value. In fact, they might be even liabilities when it comes to the most important thing in life—knowing Christ.

It's important to recognize that Paul didn't come to this understanding lightly. These privileges were important things which had impacted his life for the better. Yet, when it came to furthering and deepening his relationship with Christ, Paul recognized them for what they were—garbage. In other words, none of these assets were beneficial in helping him to "gain Christ and be found in him." Christ, Paul knew, would easily outweigh anything else that we consider of value or importance. To "know Christ" and the "power of his resurrection" is therefore the ultimate goal that Paul, the Philippians, and we should pursue. For it is only when we recognize that because Christ died, we ourselves must die to anything that keeps us from fully participating in His death in order that we can ultimately live into the "resurrection from the dead."

CHRISTLIKENESS REQUIRES EFFORT

Philippians 3:12-14

Having just described his desire to "know Christ," Paul recognizes that the Philippians might take what he has written as an indication that he has already achieved the full measure of what it means to follow Christ. Therefore, Paul states that he continues to

MODELING IS A COMMUNAL EXERCISE

"press on toward the goal." Paul makes clear that "knowing Christ" and attaining "the prize" God has for us takes great effort, time, and commitment. Coming to know Christ in His fullness is not a moment-in-time issue, but rather a life-long pursuit.

To "press on toward the goal" requires two things: 1) "forgetting what is behind," and 2) "straining toward what is ahead." Paul emphasizes both pieces are critical. The past must be forgotten. This is not a one-time action, but a continual process. It is not just about forgetting the bad things, but also recognizing not to dwell on the good things, which may keep us from looking forward.

We are also called to "strain" toward what is ahead. This is not a casual attempt to follow Jesus. Rather, this implies that we only have eyes for what is ahead of us, the prize which is Christ. Our total concentration is on what it means to seek after the knowledge of Christ. As we do this, we recognize we are no longer focused on ourselves but on Christ alone.

BECOMING MORE LIKE CHRIST
Philippians 3:15-16

Paul uses a play on words here when he says that all "who are mature should take such a view of things." Earlier Paul talked about how he had not "already arrived at the goal" of knowing all about Christ (the word "arrived" is often translated "perfect"). Here Paul uses the same word (translated as "mature" here), but with irony. Anyone who considers himself/herself perfect should recognize that perfection isn't the current state in which we find ourselves, but the pursuit of what we are becoming. This is the perfection, this constant pursuit of Christ, that we should live into.

Philippians 3:17

Paul now exhorts his brothers and sisters in Christ to emulate him as he pursues Christ. What the Philippians are to model is not Paul's achievements or privileges. Instead, they are to model his self-abandonment, his willingness to suffer on behalf of others, his humility, and his passionate pursuit of Jesus. This is no solo endeavor. Rather, it is an invitation to communally follow in his steps, to see how the community seeks the heart of Jesus.

HAVING THE PROPER MOTIVATION MATTERS
Philippians 3:18-21

Paul is adamant that the Philippians follow his pattern for living because he recognizes there are others who call themselves Christians who do not embody these same principles. Paul recognizes that their desires and underlying motives don't lead them to the same goal of fully knowing Christ in His death and suffering. Instead, by modeling the attitudes and practices that Paul embodies, the Philippians will be living out what it means to be a citizen of the kingdom of God. Both Paul and the Philippians do this because they eagerly await the coming again of their Savior who will ultimately deliver them not only from their opponents, but also the sufferings which they face. When He comes, all the sufferings the Philippians have faced will be redeemed, healed, and transformed for His sake. This will be part of the "prize" that Paul and the Philippians will win because they were faithful and passionate in their pursuit of Christ.

REFLECT In what ways are you pressing forward toward the goal on your spiritual journey?

JIM HAMPTON

29

REJOICE IN THE LORD

Believers have many reasons to be joyful.

THE WORD

PHILIPPIANS 4:4-13

KEY VERSE

Rejoice in the Lord always. I will say it again: Rejoice! ⁵Let your gentleness be evident to all. The Lord is near. ⁶Do not be anxious about anything, but in every situation, by prayer and petition, with thanksgiving, present your requests to God. ⁷And the peace of God, which transcends all understanding, will guard your hearts and your minds in Christ Jesus.

⁸Finally, brothers and sisters, whatever is true, whatever is noble, whatever is right, whatever is pure, whatever is lovely, whatever is admirable—if anything is excellent or praiseworthy—think about such things. ⁹Whatever you have learned or received or heard from me, or seen in me—put it into practice. And the God of peace will be with you.

¹⁰I rejoiced greatly in the Lord that at last you renewed your concern for me. Indeed, you were concerned, but you had no opportunity to show it. ¹¹I am not saying this because I am in need, for I have learned to be content whatever the circumstances. ¹²I know what it is to be in need, and I know what it is to have plenty. I have learned the secret of being content in any and every situation, whether well fed or hungry, whether living in plenty or in want. ¹³I can do all this through him who gives me strength.

ENGAGE THE WORD

JOY AND REJOICING

Philippians 4:4-7

The words "joy" and "rejoicing" occur 16 times in this brief letter, so it should be no surprise that this is a concept Paul wants to emphasize. For Paul, joy is living with a resolved mind that is distinguished by peace. This does not mean that Paul was not impacted by the hardships around him. Throughout this letter he's described the numerous sufferings both he and the Philippians have endured. These sufferings would surely have produced sorrow, pain, and disappointment. Yet, even so, Paul admonishes the Philippians to "rejoice!" Therefore, for Paul joy is more than happiness (a mood or emotion that is based on current circumstances). Instead, it is the recognition that God is in control, and we can trust in His good will. Joy allows us to see beyond the current external forces and instead focus on the One who has sovereign control over life.

Paul's command to "rejoice" is a habitual action that the Philippians are to engage in, knowing that the more they practice joy, the more it will change how they see the world around them. This keeps joy from being fleeting, and instead it becomes ingrained in their very core.

When lives are lived with joy, Paul says, then gentleness will be the normative response to others. The word "gentleness" carries with it a sense of generosity in how we deal with others. Being gentle with others means we don't seek our rights if that means the other is negatively impacted. And the result of this life of gentleness, Paul proclaims, is that everyone around us, both saint and sinner, will see it and recognize it as being of God.

Paul then makes an exclamation, "The Lord is near." This phrase has two possible meanings. One, God is close by, walking with Paul and the Philippians, seeking to provide them what they need to faithfully journey together. Second, Paul could be implying that

Did You Know?

The list of virtues Paul presents for the Philippians to ponder would have been widely known and practiced by the wider society (v. 8). Many philosophers of the day would have encouraged their followers to adopt these same virtues. In including them here, Paul is reminding the Philippians that they live in the larger society, and not only should they recognize the aphorism that "all truth is God's truth, regardless of the source," but that absolute moral standards do exist and that even non-Christians may practice them. The thrust then is Paul desires that the Philippians can benefit from pondering these virtues.

the return of Jesus is near. Thus, their gentleness is an opportunity for others to come to know the Lord before Christ returns.

Paul gives yet another set of exhortations: "Stop worrying, pray with thanksgiving!" Paul recognized the human tendency to worry needlessly over things beyond our control. And the reality was, both Paul and the Philippians had lots of reasons to worry. Paul was imprisoned and the Philippians were facing significant persecution. Yet, even so, Paul reminds them that as great as their worries may be, God is greater.

Instead of worrying, Paul instructs them to bring all those worries to God. Their anxiety over the things they faced would be lessened by bringing everything-—prayers, petitions, and requests—to God. Paul knew that the more they spent time in prayer asking God to address these issues, the less they would feel stressed and frightened. He desired that the Philippians would be able to offer to the Creator of the universe their concerns, their needs, their desires, and believe that He in turn would enable them to live in a state of peace. It is a peace which reflects the way God exists—a tranquility of spirit that enables the Philippians to not be frazzled by life's circumstances.

FOCUS OUR MINDS

Philippians 4:8-9

Here Paul offers one last imperative for the Philippians. As important as living a life characterized by joy, peace, and prayer enables one to stand firm, so too should the Philippians focus their minds on the virtues of the Christian life. An actual inventory of our thoughts might reveal doubts, harsh judgments, irrational assumptions, and so on. Paul's list speaks to what we should be filling our minds with. Paul claims that when the Philippians ponder and live out these virtues it is all done under the lordship of the God of peace. These virtues originate from God's very character, which makes their practice all the more important.

Unit 1: Philippians

However, it's not enough just to consider these virtues. Paul goes on to say that the Philippians need to embody them. As they consider Paul's life, they should see the virtues expressed in his words and actions. Therefore, using Paul as an exemplar of sorts, they should endeavor to live out these virtues in the same way they've seen Paul do so.

A WORD OF THANKS
Philippians 4:10-13

Paul concludes this passage by naming his thanks for the Philippians generous gift sent via Epaphroditus. Paul states that while he did not need the gift, he is overjoyed at the sacrificial nature of it, as it demonstrates who they are—a people committed to offering self-giving love to those who need it.

Why is it that Paul does not need their gift? It is because he has "learned the secret of being content in any and every situation." Paul suggests that he has learned to be content regardless of the particular circumstances in which he finds himself—"whether well fed or hungry, whether living in plenty or in want." While the concept of self-sufficiency was something that the philosophers of the day practiced, Paul takes the concept and places it squarely under the lordship of Christ. The only way he can learn to truly be content is not because of his own abilities or discipline, but because "I can do all this through him who gives me strength." The discipline he has learned is how to rely and trust on God alone to supply his needs.

Think About It
There is a tendency among many Christians to read Paul's statement, "I have learned to be content whatever the circumstances" as being about self-sufficiency. But in this passage, Paul is stating that he is content only because God supplies his needs. Note that the Philippians were part of that response. So, to say we are content is to recognize not only God's work to meet our needs, but the people that God uses, and to see them as an indispensable element of being content.

REFLECT In what way do you need God's peace in your life today?

JIM HAMPTON

CELEBRATING REDEMPTION

God has provided for us salvation in Christ Jesus.

THE WORD

EPHESIANS 1:1-14

Paul, an apostle of Christ Jesus by the will of God,

To God's holy people in Ephesus, the faithful in Christ Jesus:

²Grace and peace to you from God our Father and the Lord Jesus Christ.

³Praise be to the God and Father of our Lord Jesus Christ, who has blessed us in the heavenly realms with every spiritual blessing in Christ. ⁴For he chose us in him before the creation of the world to be holy and blameless in his sight. In love ⁵he predestined us for adoption to sonship through Jesus Christ, in accordance with his pleasure and will—⁶to the praise of his glorious grace, which he has freely given us in the One he loves.

KEY VERSES

⁷In him we have redemption through his blood, the forgiveness of sins, in accordance with the riches of God's grace ⁸that he lavished on us. With all wisdom and understanding, ⁹he made known to us the mystery of his will according to his good pleasure, which he purposed in Christ, ¹⁰to be put into effect when the times reach their fulfillment—to bring unity to all things in heaven and on earth under Christ.

¹¹In him we were also chosen, having been predestined according to the plan of him who works out everything in conformity with the purpose of his will, ¹²in order that we, who were the first to put our hope in Christ, might be for the praise of his glory. ¹³And you also were included in Christ when you heard the message of truth, the gospel of your salvation. When you believed, you were marked in him with a seal, the promised Holy Spirit, ¹⁴who is a deposit guaranteeing our inheritance until the redemption of those who are God's possession—to the praise of his glory.

ENGAGE THE WORD

PAUL'S LETTER TO GOD'S HOLY PEOPLE

Ephesians 1:1-2

Paul identified himself to his readers as an apostle (literally, "sent-out one") or representative of Christ Jesus "by the will of God." Paul addressed his letter to "God's holy people," whom he also described as "the faithful in Christ Jesus." "Holy" carries a dual meaning of "set apart" and "morally pure." God's intention for believers is for them to be set apart both for His service and for moral purity or holiness. This kind of set-apart holiness is only possible inasmuch as a believer is "in Christ Jesus" because of their ongoing faith in Christ alone. For Paul, all the blessings and promises of God are possible only through the believers' relationship to God "in Christ."

Paul greeted his readers with his desire for "grace and peace" to be fully realized in their lives. Grace conveys the idea of God's unmerited favor, while peace describes well-being or wholeness of life. Both terms emphasize God's initial salvation as well as His ongoing work in the lives of His people in and through Christ.

GOD'S PLAN OF SALVATION IN CHRIST FROM THE BEGINNING

Ephesians 1:3-6

After his greeting, Paul launched into a beautiful hymn of praise consisting of a single Greek sentence that extends from verses 3-14. Paul praised God for the spiritual blessings of Christ. Literally, verse 3 reads, "Blessed be God...who has blessed us...with every spiritual blessing in Christ." Paul identified "in Christ" as the qualifying and descriptive foundation of God's plan and purpose for the salvation of all believers. Paul's understanding that salvation is found only "in Christ" is reinforced by his use of this phrase 36 times in Ephesians.

It was always God's plan "before the creation of the world" (v. 4) that salvation would be facilitated through faith in Christ and an ongoing relationship with Him. The phrases "he chose us" (v. 4) and "he predestined us" (v. 5) reflect election language to underscore the reality that God took the initiative in making salvation possible. God loved first, God chose first, God acted first. When the topic of election comes up, people often think of the election of individuals and the personal benefits of salvation. But the plural pronouns "us" demonstrate that Paul is thinking in corporate terms of the "church" or "God's people," and not of individuals. From the beginning of time, God's election consisted of Christ as the means of salvation to all who would believe. The identity of the elect is determined by those who respond positively to God's invitation to be saved by faith in Jesus Christ. Believers must cooperate with God's grace by placing their faith in Jesus in order to be saved.

Election also brings responsibility. God chose us (the church) to do something; namely, He chose us to live holy and blameless lives before Him (v. 4). It is only appropriate that a holy God would call to himself a holy people of His own. Thus, God's love compelled Him to design a "predestined" plan even before the creation of the world to adopt into His chosen family whoever believes in Jesus Christ.

The basis of our salvation is God's glorious grace and love, which He has freely given us in Christ (v. 6). Because of this glorious revealing of God's grace and love in Jesus Christ, God is worthy of our eternal praise.

REDEMPTION AND UNITY IN CHRIST

Ephesians 1:7-10

God is not only worthy of praise for what He has done in the past, but also for what He is currently doing in the lives of people through His grace. Paul reminded his readers that in Christ, "we have redemption through his blood" (v. 7). The verb "have" is present tense, which connotes an ongoing action in the present time. The blessings and plan that God preordained from the very beginning of time became a present reality in the cross of Jesus.

HOLY SPIRIT AS SEAL AND DEPOSIT

In Christ, we have redemption. Literally, redemption means "release by ransom," and was used for buying back a slave or captive and setting them free. At the cost of His own blood and life, Christ made redemption possible for those who believe in Him. The result is the forgiveness of sins, which underscores the reality that God has "let go" or "set aside" the just punishment that our transgressions rightfully deserve. Instead of convicting believers with the punishment their sins deserve, God has set aside our sins and forgiven us because of what Christ has done for us on the cross. This is the essence of grace, which is part of the mystery God put into action in Christ. God's divine plan from the very beginning was to redeem, forgive, and restore all things into a heavenly unity of purpose in and through Christ so that all creation might be united to declare the praise of God's "glorious grace" (vv. 6, 12, 14).

Ephesians 1:11-14

God's plan is that every person who puts their hope and faith in Christ, including both the Jew and the Gentile, is "included in Christ" and becomes a recipient of the blessings and promises of God (v. 13). Even though believers experience many of the blessings of God now already, they have not yet received their promised inheritance. Thus, God has given His promised Holy Spirit as a deposit guaranteeing the blessings that are yet to come in the future. As the "guarantee of our inheritance" (v. 14), the Spirit leads Christ's followers to live out the reality of God's promised deliverance in a life that brings praise to the glory of God.

REFLECT Consider what it means for you to be "in Christ."

DANIEL G. POWERS is the director of the Pastoral Ministries program and professor of New Testament at Nazarene Bible College. He is also the author of *1, 2 Peter and Jude* in the *New Beacon Bible Commentary* series. He and his wife Mieke live in Colorado Springs, CO.

RESURRECTION POWER

As we know God better, we experience the power of Christ at work in our lives.

THE WORD

EPHESIANS 1:15-23

For this reason, ever since I heard about your faith in the Lord Jesus and your love for all God's people, [16]I have not stopped giving thanks for you, remembering you in my prayers. [17]I keep asking that the God of our Lord Jesus Christ, the glorious Father, may give you the Spirit of wisdom and revelation, so that you may know him better.

KEY VERSES

[18]**I pray that the eyes of your heart may be enlightened in order that you may know the hope to which he has called you, the riches of his glorious inheritance in his holy people, [19]and his incomparably great power for us who believe. That power is the same as the mighty strength [20]he exerted when he raised Christ from the dead and seated him at his right hand in the heavenly realms,** [21]far above all rule and authority, power and dominion, and every name that is invoked, not only in the present age but also in the one to come. [22]And God placed all things under his feet and appointed him to be head over everything for the church, [23]which is his body, the fullness of him who fills everything in every way.

ENGAGE THE WORD

NEWS OF FAITH AND LOVE LEADS TO THANKSGIVING

Ephesians 1:15-16

Two elements prompted Paul's thanksgiving for his readers. First, "for this reason" reveals that Paul's thanksgiving bubbled up out of his praise to God for the spiritual blessings God had made possible for believers in Christ through the work of the Holy Spirit (1:3-14). Second, Paul's thanks were induced by the report he received about their faith in Jesus and

Unit 2: Ephesians

their love for other believers. God's spiritual blessings lead to faith in Christ which inevitably leads Christians to love other believers, who are described here as God's people. The reports of their faith and love provided evidence that the spiritual blessings of God were taking root and growing in their lives. This news prompted Paul to give thanks and to lift them up in his prayers.

PAUL'S PRAYER FOR BELIEVERS

Ephesians 1:17-19a

After giving thanks for them, Paul prays for them. Paul's prayer was that God would reveal to them the incredible blessings they have in Christ so that they may know God better. We should notice the Trinitarian nature of the dynamic power that is at work in believers. God is not only the God of our Lord Jesus Christ, but also "the glorious Father" (v. 17). As the "glorious Father," God is not only the Father to whom all glory belongs, but also the Father from whom all glory comes. Glory here emphasizes radiance and majesty, but it is also a synonym for power to accomplish the will and purposes of the Father. Likewise, Jesus is identified as Christ, but also as Lord and Master. One of the earliest confessions was the proclamation that Jesus is Lord, or that Jesus is our Lord. As Lord, Jesus is the Master and Savior of those who believe in Him for salvation. Finally, the Trinitarian triad is completed with the Spirit of wisdom and revelation. It is the "wise Spirit" who reveals God's glorious purposes and blessings to the world in Christ. Those who recognize the spiritual blessings God makes possible through faith in Jesus Christ are able to know God better. But it is the Holy Spirit who performs this task of enablement. Even the ability to know God better is something given to believers through grace. Thus, Paul portrays the full Godhead at work in the lives of believers so that they might know God and His salvational benefits better.

Paul went on to articulate his prayer for his readers

even more specifically (vv. 18-19a). The heart was considered to represent the entire inward being or personality of a person, including one's intellect, will, and emotions. Paul prayed that the Holy Spirit would illuminate the "heart" of the believers so they would truly know the reality of what God had accomplished for them in and through Christ. Paul's prayer for enlightenment was that his readers might know three realities about God.

First, Paul wanted them to know the hope to which God had called them (v. 18). In Greek, "hope" referred merely to an anticipation of future events of all kinds, including both good and evil. Thus, people had to stand without hope before the hostile forces of guilt and death. But because of Christ, "hope" is never used in the New Testament to indicate a vague or fearful anticipation; rather, it always denotes the expectation of something good. In this sense, God gave birth to hope for all believers in the person of Jesus our Lord! God's invitation and call to accept His saving grace makes a radical—and positive-—change in what the future holds for believers. God's call to salvation is a call to joyous and victorious hope for the future.

Second, Paul prayed for enlightenment about the "riches of his glorious inheritance in his holy people" (v. 18). God enacted every detail of His plan of salvation in Christ through the Holy Spirit in order for believers to become God's possession, God's inheritance, God's holy people. Just as the inheritance of redemption for believers is both a present reality and a future promise (1:14), so also God has set apart His people as a holy people as both a present reality and a future promise. Part of what it means for believers to be God's people is for them also to be set apart as a holy people who are blameless and righteous because of the work of Christ within them. As such, we are God's glorious inheritance by virtue of the work of Christ in us.

Third, Paul prayed that believers would recognize

Think About It
The trilogy of faith, love, and hope appears in Paul's thanksgiving prayer for his readers. Paul hears about their faith and love (v. 15) and he prays they might know the hope to which God called them.

GOD'S RESURRECTION POWER AT WORK

God's incomparably great power at work within them. Paul prayed that the believers would be able to grasp the reality that God's incomparable power was available for them as God's people in Christ.

Ephesians 1:19b-23

Paul reminded his readers that the supremely powerful God who raised Jesus from the dead and exalted Him above all things is the same God whose resurrection power is at work in the life of believers and the church. Believers must remember how the power of God raised and transformed the lowly, rejected, crucified, dead and buried Jesus up from the grave to the exalted position of power and authority at the right hand of God himself. Whatever powers might exist in the present or future, they are all subject to the exalted Christ. God placed all things under the feet of Christ and appointed Him to be the head over all things for the benefit of the church. Paul's identification of the church as the body of Christ is a vivid reminder that the power and blessings of God are reserved for individuals only inasmuch as they are united with both Christ and with the body of Christ, His church. God's power at work in believers is not intended to attain worldly gain. Instead, godly power is the power to participate and contribute in the mission of Jesus. As such, God did not plan for individual believers to possess godly power for their own spiritual benefit only. Rather, He calls and empowers believers to be a part of His holy people, the body of Christ, which is the church. It is in Christ's body-—His church—where we find and experience together the fullness of Christ who fills everything and everyone in every way.

REFLECT What does it mean to have God's resurrection power at work in your life today?

DANIEL G. POWERS

TRANSFORMING GRACE

The transforming grace of God is available and at work in all believers.

THE WORD

EPHESIANS 2:1-10

As for you, you were dead in your transgressions and sins, ²in which you used to live when you followed the ways of this world and of the ruler of the kingdom of the air, the spirit who is now at work in those who are disobedient. ³All of us also lived among them at one time, gratifying the cravings of our flesh and following its desires and thoughts. Like the rest, we were by nature deserving of

KEY VERSES

wrath. **⁴But because of his great love for us, God, who is rich in mercy, ⁵made us alive with Christ even when we were dead in transgressions—it is by grace you have been saved.** ⁶And God raised us up with Christ and seated us with him in the heavenly realms in Christ Jesus, ⁷in order that in the coming ages he might show the incomparable riches of his grace, expressed in his kindness to us in Christ Jesus. ⁸For it is by grace you have been saved, through faith—and this is not from yourselves, it is the gift of God—⁹not by works, so that no one can boast. ¹⁰For we are God's handiwork, created in Christ Jesus to do good works, which God prepared in advance for us to do.

ENGAGE THE WORD

PREVIOUSLY DEAD IN SIN

Ephesians 2:1-3

Before Christ, Paul's readers "were dead in your transgressions and sins" (v. 1). When a person has been renewed and reborn in Christ, they realize that life without Christ was a life hardly worth living. Indeed, without God, a person is spiritually dead and lifeless because of the numbing grip of sin that separates them from God. One tragic consequence of sin is that it blinds and paralyzes its victims so that they are not only powerless to escape its shackles, but they are also ignorant to their own lifeless and entrapped existence.

While the reference to "transgressions and sins" points to behavioral issues, the problem of sin lies much deeper in the realm of control or dominion. Who controls your life? Living in sin is the result of living in (literally, "walking in") the ways of this world under the "ruler of the kingdom of the air" (v. 2). This ruler is also described as "the spirit who is now at work in those who are disobedient." These phrases depict an evil, diabolical force that leads sinners to rebel against God and to reject His righteous ways. Elsewhere in Ephesians, Paul refers to a life of sin as following the evil one (6:16) or the devil (4:27; 6:11). The problem of sinners is not merely their sinful behavior, but their entrapped allegiance to the devil as their master.

Sometimes believers are tempted to look down on sinners with self-righteous notions that separate "us believers" from "those sinners." But Paul reminded his readers that "all of us also lived among them at one time" (v. 3). Before we surrendered our lives to Christ, all of us were slaves to sin and Satan. We need to remember that unbelievers are not our enemies who deserve our animosity and rejection; rather, they need our prayers and intercession on their behalf. All of us, like them, were once "by nature deserving of wrath" (v. 3).

NOW MADE ALIVE IN CHRIST

Ephesians 2:4-7

Verse 4 begins with an emphasis on God's gracious initiative. The situation seemed bleak and hopeless, but God responded to the sinner's predicament with love and mercy. What an incredible contrast between what someone deserves versus what they receive from God! Instead of treating sin with the wrath it deserved, God responded with love and mercy. Mercy and love are reflections of God's inherent being and nature. Mercy can be defined as kindness or concern expressed for someone in need. God's mercy flows out of His love (literally, "his great love with which he loved us"), and it reveals His unique way of reaching out to help those who are totally undeserving.

God's love and mercy became vividly visible in the reality that, even when we were dead in sin, God "made us alive with Christ" (v. 5). This is what grace looks like, and it results in life and salvation instead of death and condemnation.

In verses 5-7, Paul repeatedly employs the phrases "with Christ" and "in Christ" to underscore the reality that salvation is the result of the believer's ongoing solidarity and union with Christ. Even though they were once dead in sin, believers are now alive with Christ and raised up with Christ into the heavenly realms as a witness to the world of God's incomparable grace and kindness. God demonstrated His great mercy and love by reaching out to sinners in love, even while they were still lost and enslaved in sin and rebellion. This is what Paul meant when he wrote that "it is by grace you have been saved" (v. 5). Salvation is the result of God's grace, which prompted Him to pour out undeserved mercy and love on those who are united with Christ.

SAVED BY GRACE THROUGH FAITH TO SERVE

Ephesians 2:8-10

But how are believers united with Christ and saved? It is by God's grace that sinners are saved, through their faith in Jesus Christ (v. 8). While God's grace is the

Think About It

Ephesians 2:1-10 is one of many biblical passages supporting the doctrine of "prevenient grace." Prevenient grace refers to God's grace taking the initiative in drawing sinners to himself even while they are dead in their transgressions. God in Christ always makes the first move.

only true source of salvation, faith is the only means by which salvation can be received and retained. We are not saved by our faith, but by grace through faith. However, both grace and faith are gifts of God. Even the ability to have faith in Christ for salvation is a gift of God; thus, there are no grounds for boasting. Nonetheless, faith is required for salvation as an act of acceptance and surrender to God. God will not save anyone against their will. There must be a human response of surrender and acceptance of God's free gift in order for God to activate His grace into saving grace.

Ultimately, the reason why no one can boast about their acceptance of God's grace through faith is because "we are God's handiwork." Literally, "handiwork" means "that which is made, work, creation." Paul considered salvation to be part of God's "new creation." The believer's "new creation" is the result of God's work and activity, not our own work.

Finally, the purpose of God's grace was not merely so that sinners could be saved. Rather, believers are masterful new creations in Christ Jesus in order to perform good works, which God prepared in advance for them to do. We are not saved by good works, but we are saved for good works. Good works do not earn one's salvation, but they are an essential and natural by-product of one's new life in Christ Jesus. Once again, the contrast of the believer's life before and after salvation is very striking. Whereas the spiritually dead walk and live in disobedience and sin (2:1, 2), those who are made alive with Christ are a new creation who walk and live a life filled with good works (v. 10).

REFLECT Take time this week to thank God for His love, mercy, and grace.

DANIEL G. POWERS

UNITED IN CHRIST

The unity we have in Christ supersedes all our differences.

THE WORD

EPHESIANS 2:11-22

Therefore, remember that formerly you who are Gentiles by birth and called "uncircumcised" by those who call themselves "the circumcision" (which is done in the body by human hands)—[12]remember that at that time you were separate from Christ, excluded from citizenship in Israel and foreigners to the covenants of the promise, without hope and without God in the world. [13]But now in Christ Jesus you who once were far away have been brought near by the blood of Christ.

[14]For he himself is our peace, who has made the two groups one and has destroyed the barrier, the dividing wall of hostility, [15]by setting aside in his flesh the law with its commands and regulations. His purpose was to create in himself one new humanity out of the two, thus making peace, [16]and in one body to reconcile both of them to God through the cross, by which he put to death their hostility. [17]He came and preached peace to you who were far away and peace to those who were near. [18]For through him we both have access to the Father by one Spirit.

KEY VERSES **[19]Consequently, you are no longer foreigners and strangers, but fellow citizens with God's people and also members of his household, [20]built on the foundation of the apostles and prophets, with Christ Jesus himself as the chief cornerstone.** [21]In him the whole building is joined together and rises to become a holy temple in the Lord. [22]And in him you too are being built together to become a dwelling in which God lives by his Spirit.

ENGAGE THE WORD

ONCE FAR AWAY, NOW BROUGHT NEAR

Ephesians 2:11-13

In Ephesians 2:1-10, Paul reminded his Gentile readers of the miraculous change Christ made possible in their life. Whereas they were once "dead in your trespasses and sins" (2:1), they were now "alive in Christ" because of God's mercy and grace (2:4-5). Salvation through faith in Jesus brought not only forgiveness of sins, but also reconciliation with God.

Beginning in 2:11, Paul reminded his readers again about the painful reality of their life before Christ. Within the Jewish world, Gentiles by definition were considered to be sinners (Galatians 2:15), while the Jewish people prided themselves as being God's chosen people. The separation between Jew and Gentile was punctuated even more dramatically by the physical mark of circumcision on the bodies of the Jewish men. With derision, the Jews insulted the Gentiles as the "uncircumcised," and avoided Gentiles as much as possible.

Paul urged his readers to be mindful of their former life before Christ. They were not only separated from the Jews, but they were separated from God. As such, they were excluded from God's people. They were strangers and foreigners to God, unaware of the promises of God's covenant with His people. Before Christ, they were cut off from faith and from "God's people." Their citizenship was not in the kingdom of God. Indeed, before Christ, they were "without hope and without God in the world" (2:12).

But now, everything changed because of Christ. Using his favorite phrase "in Christ," Paul reminded his readers of their new status "now in Christ Jesus." The before-and-after contrast could not be more pronounced. While their former lives of sin and rebellion had pushed them far away from God, the covenant, the promises of blessing, and even from hope itself, they had now been brought near by the life-giving, atoning blood of Christ. God's grace is nowhere more

THE RECONCILING POWER OF CHRIST, OUR PEACE

evident than in the fact that Christ died for those who were far away in order to bring them near to God's throne of grace and salvation.

Ephesians 2:14-18

Paul reminded the Ephesians that Christ is our peace. This is a different reality than the statement that Christ "brings about" peace. Christ alone is the source, the origin, and the provider of peace. In Greek and English, the basic meaning of "peace" can be boiled down to the idea of the absence or end of hostility or war. But the peace Christ represents is not merely the Greek idea of the ending of hostilities; rather, it is the Hebrew idea of *shalom,* an all-embracing term that describes salvation and life with God. This is the kind of peace that Christ represents.

The reconciliation between different peoples (like Jews and Gentiles) and between people and God happens only in Christ. Christ has taken all the barriers, walls, distinctions, and hostilities that sin has created between God and people and between peoples themselves and has put them to death in His own body through the cross. By doing this, Christ destroyed the barriers that sin created between Jews and Gentiles and every other sinful division of people; He made reconciliation with God possible for all people through faith and obedience to Jesus Christ. In other words, Christ created in himself one new humanity in which there are no longer any barriers or divisions. This is what the peace of Christ looks like in action. Divided humanity is reconciled in Christ, and in His "one body" they become a worshiping community that is also reconciled to God. This "one body" is represented by the church, where Christ makes "insiders" out of those who were formerly "outsiders" so that through Christ every person can have access to the Father by the one Spirit. Indeed, this has always been God's intention for His people, which is represented in the church, the body of Christ, where

Unit 2: Ephesians

peace with God and peace with other people is made possible.

Ephesians 2:19-22

In Christ a new citizenship is formed. Sin separated different nationalities and ethnic groups into opposing entities of outsiders and insiders. But Christ, through His death and resurrection, dismantled the dividing wall and created a new people, whom Paul described as fellow citizens, God's people (literally, "holy ones"), and members of God's household (v. 19). As fellow residents in God's household, there are no longer "Jewish Christians" and "Gentile Christians." In Christ, we are all just "Christians."

The imagery of the church as God's household in verse 19 allowed Paul to make an easy transition to describing the construction of the building or house in which families lived. The foundation of this house is nothing other than the teaching of Scripture, which is described as "the foundation of the apostles and prophets" (v. 20). Whenever the values, focus, or preaching of a church lose their firm footing in Scripture, the basis of its very existence is undermined and destroyed. The bedrock on which the family of God lives in peace and unity is found in Scripture, and Jesus himself is the chief cornerstone. This is where the presence of God is vibrant, growing, and life-transforming through the ongoing work of God's Holy Spirit. As the household of God, the church is the community where all people, regardless of their separate and diverse backgrounds, are able to become God's holy people, united together in Christ.

Think About It

The phrase "in Christ" occurs 36 times in Ephesians and seven times in verses 11-22. Paul is emphasizing that everything of significance for faith takes place "in Christ."

FELLOW CITIZENS IN THE FAMILY OF GOD

REFLECT What does it mean to be a citizen in the family of God?

DANIEL G. POWERS

MATURITY IN THE BODY

The body of Christ should seek and exhibit harmony and maturity.

THE WORD

EPHESIANS 4:1-16

As a prisoner for the Lord, then, I urge you to live a life worthy of the calling you have received. [2]Be completely humble and gentle; be patient, bearing with one another in love. [3]Make every effort to keep the unity of the Spirit through the bond of peace. [4]There is one body and one Spirit, just as you were called to one hope when you were called; [5]one Lord, one faith, one baptism; [6]one God and Father of all, who is over all and through all and in all.

[7]But to each one of us grace has been given as Christ apportioned it. [8]This is why it says: "When he ascended on high, he took many captives and gave gifts to his people."

[9](What does "he ascended" mean except that he also descended to the lower, earthly regions? [10]He who descended is the very one who ascended higher than all the heavens, in order to fill the whole universe.) [11]So Christ himself gave the apostles, the prophets, the evangelists, the pastors and teachers, [12]to equip his people for works of service, so that the body of Christ may be built up [13]until we all reach unity in the faith and in the knowledge of the Son of God and become mature, attaining to the whole measure of the fullness of Christ.

[14]Then we will no longer be infants, tossed back and forth by the waves, and blown here and there by every wind of teaching and by the cunning and craftiness of people in their deceitful scheming.

KEY VERSE

[15]Instead, speaking the truth in love, we will grow to become in every respect the mature body of him who is the head, that is, Christ. [16]From him the whole body, joined and held together by every supporting ligament, grows and builds itself up in love, as each part does its work.

Unit 2: Ephesians

ENGAGE THE WORD

HARMONY IN THE BODY OF CHRIST

Ephesians 4:1-6

Paul often referred to the Christian church of the first century as the body of Christ. He presented an extended illustration of comparing the various parts of a human body to the varied members of the body of Christ in 1 Corinthians 12. He points out that the human body has many different parts. They look and function differently from one another, yet they all work together in harmony to assist a person in daily life. One body part is not more important than another.

With that illustration in mind, we can better understand Paul's message to the Ephesian believers. He offers them goals for which to strive as they live as individual members in one spiritual body. This body should "live a life worthy of the calling you have received" (4:1), with humility, gentleness, patience, and forbearance. Members of the body of Christ must function together as one since every aspect of the Christian faith is unified. That is, one body, one Spirit, one hope, one Lord, one faith, one baptism, and one God and Father is over all. The unity between the Father, Son, and Holy Spirit models unity in the body of Christ on earth. God wants the body of Christ to show the world how His children live together as Jews, Gentiles, rich, disenfranchised, educated, uneducated, extraverts, introverts, and so on. God is one and so His church should function together as one.

MATURE DIVERSITY

Ephesians 4:7-13

The key word in this passage appears in verse 13: mature. The ideal body of Christ on earth that Paul envisioned in the previous section can become a reality only as individual members exercise maturity in their faith. Members mature as they live into the grace Christ offers them. Christ came down from His heavenly home to live with humanity for 33 years and redeem His creation (John 1:14). He humbly modeled

Many Jewish leaders in Paul's day and many Christians throughout church history have looked at the effects of sin and godlessness in our world and written it off as beyond hope. Such pessimism led to inaction. Paul offered the church a hopeful message through the redemption in Christ Jesus and the transforming power of the Holy Spirit to make the body of Christ a light in our sin darkened world.

in daily life all of the Christian virtues Paul listed in verses 2-3 (Philippians 2:6-11).

More than simply modeling these virtues, Christ gives every member of His body on earth the gifts and graces needed to excel in the ministries to which He calls them. Christ calls and commissions them to their various leadership roles. The apostles, prophets, evangelists, pastors, and teachers each have their own assigned divine calling.

The original use of the term "apostle" in the New Testament referred to eyewitnesses of Christ's ministry, death, and resurrection. Later, however, it came to include church planters, leaders, and administrators who functioned as apostles. Paul included himself in that description. Prophets proclaimed God's plan of redemption by grace through faith in Jesus Christ. Evangelists have the special gift of preaching the gospel message to those who have never heard it. Missionaries are often evangelists who preach and teach the gospel message in cross-cultural settings. Pastors shepherd the flock within the community of faith with preaching, support, counseling, and protection from the spiritual scams of the world. Teachers give instruction and deeper understanding to Scripture, the doctrines of the Christian faith, and ethical practices for living blamelessly in sin-filled world.

Each of these church leaders minister both to pre-believers in the world and especially to believers so they can "equip his people for works of service" (Ephesians 4:12). They train and mentor every member of the community of faith for the work to which Christ has called them. No ministry assignment is more important than another just as no member of the human body has superior status. Diversity of gifts and abilities continue to exist among the various members of the body of Christ. With time and practice, through the grace of Christ and the unity of the Holy Spirit, the body functions with a mature diversity "attaining to the whole measure of the fullness of Christ" (Ephesians 4:13).

Think About It

Paul stated God's eternal plan as, "to be put into effect when the times reach their fulfillment—to bring unity to all things in heaven and on earth under Christ" (Ephesians 1:10). Harmony and maturity in the body of Christ support that plan.

LOVE ABOVE ALL

Ephesians 4:14-16

Ephesians 4:1-16 begins and ends with a call for everything to be done in a spirit of love (vv. 2, 15). Members of the body can hone their ministry skills and abilities to the point of perfect execution. However, unless they minister together in love for one another and the world, their work will be hollow and temporary.

Maturing believers must remain childlike as Jesus admonished, "Truly I tell you, unless you change and become like little children, you will never enter the kingdom of heaven" (Matt 18:3). At the same time, maturing believers must not be childish as Paul warned in verse 14. Immature believers who do not study Scripture carefully and learn orthodox doctrine from mature believers can be easily scammed into following false teachers.

The unity, harmony, and maturity to which Paul called Ephesian believers provide the environment for them to live, believe, and speak the truth of the gospel message in love. This environment nurtures growth in Christlikeness. As the community of faith lives into the truth of the gospel message, they look and act more like the Christ they worship and serve. This does not mean, of course, that spiritual growth in the body of Christ makes every member exactly like another. Every person remains a unique individual. However, Christ works in each one and helps everyone grow in harmony and maturity. As Christ blesses the members of His body, the entire community of faith grows and matures corporately. Verse 16 emphasizes again that all this occurs as the unconditional love of God empowers believers.

REFLECT In what ways can a believer sow seeds of harmony within the body of Christ?

FRANK MOORE is retired General Editor for the Church of the Nazarene.

IMITATORS OF GOD

As believers imitate Christ, they become a light in their world.

THE WORD

EPHESIANS 5:1-20

KEY VERSES

Follow God's example, therefore, as dearly loved children ²and walk in the way of love, just as Christ loved us and gave himself up for us as a fragrant offering and sacrifice to God.

³But among you there must not be even a hint of sexual immorality, or of any kind of impurity, or of greed, because these are improper for God's holy people. ⁴Nor should there be obscenity, foolish talk or coarse joking, which are out of place, but rather thanksgiving. ⁵For of this you can be sure: No immoral, impure or greedy person—such a person is an idolater—has any inheritance in the kingdom of Christ and of God. ⁶Let no one deceive you with empty words, for because of such things God's wrath comes on those who are disobedient. ⁷Therefore do not be partners with them.

⁸For you were once darkness, but now you are light in the Lord. Live as children of light ⁹(for the fruit of the light consists in all goodness, righteousness and truth) ¹⁰and find out what pleases the Lord. ¹¹Have nothing to do with the fruitless deeds of darkness, but rather expose them. ¹²It is shameful even to mention what the disobedient do in secret. ¹³But everything exposed by the light becomes visible—and everything that is illuminated becomes a light. ¹⁴This is why it is said: "Wake up, sleeper, rise from the dead, and Christ will shine on you."

¹⁵Be very careful, then, how you live—not as unwise but as wise, ¹⁶making the most of every opportunity, because the days are evil. ¹⁷Therefore do not be foolish, but understand what the Lord's will is. ¹⁸Do not get drunk on wine, which leads to debauchery. Instead, be filled with the Spirit, ¹⁹speaking to one another with psalms, hymns,

and songs from the Spirit. Sing and make music from your heart to the Lord, [20]always giving thanks to God the Father for everything, in the name of our Lord Jesus Christ.

ENGAGE THE WORD

IMITATORS OF GOD

Ephesians 5:1-7

Ephesians 5:1 often shocks believers when they read it. How can a mere human being imitate the Almighty Sovereign of the universe? This is the only place in the Bible where believers are admonished to "follow God's example." Jesus, however, implied the same admonition in the Sermon on the Mount: "Be perfect, therefore, as your heavenly Father is perfect" (Matthew 5:48). Paul states clearly that God wants us to follow His example (vv. 2-7).

Our heavenly Father does not intend for us to figure out for ourselves how to follow Him. He gives us a model—His Son Jesus Christ. Christ loved us and taught us to love the Father and one another. We must follow His example and give ourselves sacrificially in service to God for non-Christians as well as members of the community of faith.

Living as imitators of our heavenly Father—as God's holy people—we cleanse our lives of all sinful actions and speech (vv. 3-5). Patterns of our old sinful lifestyle may be ingrained in muscle memory in such a way that old habits seek to follow us into our new life in Christ. The cleansing and transforming power of God, however, makes us a new creation (2 Corinthians 5:17). Therefore, our conduct and speech must now fill the air with the aroma of love, blessing, and thanksgiving (2 Corinthians 2:15). We must also guard against being led astray by false teachers who distort the gospel message (vv. 6-7).

CHILDREN OF LIGHT

Ephesians 5:8-14

The Bible often contrasts the difference between light and darkness. Paul uses this contrast as a metaphor describing the radical difference between our old life of sin and our new life in Christ. We once wandered aimlessly in darkness (vv. 8, 11); now we live in the light of the Lord (vv. 8, 9, 13). Living in the light describes not only our intimate relationship with God, but also our daily conduct. Children of the light bear the fruit of "goodness, righteousness, and truth" as they grow in a lifestyle pleasing to the Lord (vv. 9-10). This growth does not require slavish adherence to a long list of ethical practices to either model or reject. Rather, growth occurs naturally, like the by-product of good fruit from a healthy tree, through daily fellowship with God (Galatians 5:25; Ephesians 3:16-21).

Children of light testify to the life-changing power of God's work in them. Light and darkness are mutually exclusive; they cannot occupy the same space at the same time. So, when children of light encounter those choosing to live in darkness, they expose the utter bankruptcy of living in the fruitlessness of darkness. Paul says we do not need to specifically identify deeds of darkness (v. 11); they include all lifestyle choices that disrespect and dishonor God's will and way. Those who choose to live in darkness willfully break God's law and heart.

We must always remember that children of light do not produce their own light. Rather, they reflect the light of Jesus Christ through their relationship with Him (v. 14). He alone is the light of the world.

SPIRIT-FILLED BELIEVERS

Ephesians 5:15-20

This section of Paul's letter offers a sobering imperative: "Be very careful, then, how you live—not as unwise but as wise" (v. 15). Along with choosing each day to live as children of light in making moral choices, we must also make wise decisions. That is, we must be good stewards of the time God gives us to live in this world. Each day of believers' lives comes as a gift from God and an opportunity to worship and please Him. The contrast between wise and unwise decisions calls believers to always seek to do the Lord's will. How do

Unit 2: Ephesians

Think About It

"Jesus did not die only that Christians might live, but to show them how to live sacrificial lives (see Phil 4:18). Love and forgiveness were costly for Christ, and so it is for those who would follow him" (*NBBC: Ephesianss, Colossians, Philemon* [Kansas City: Beacon Hill Press of Kansas City, 2019], 172).

believers discern the Lord's will? Paul gives the answer in verse 18: "Be filled with the Spirit."

Those who live in darkness choose to dull their senses from the bankruptcy of their lives by getting drunk on wine. This ritual of persistent drunkenness becomes a common coping mechanism of darkness dwellers. That was not only a default choice in Bible times, it remains a common choice of those who live in darkness today. (Case in point: During the global isolation of the COVID-19 pandemic, the sale of wine, liquor, and drugs reached new highs.)

Children of light, on the other hand, live transformed lives as they are filled with the Spirit. Some biblical references to Spirit-filling describe a moment in time event (Acts 2:1-4; 10:44; 19:6). However, in verse 18 Paul used a present tense verb—"be *continually* filled with the Spirit" (italics added). The Holy Spirit does not simply visit believers occasionally. Rather, He lives daily in their hearts and lives as they remain open to God's work in them.

The fullness of the Holy Spirit in believers leads them to serve God in a variety of ways. They speak and sing together the psalms and songs of the faith (v. 19). They thank God for everything. And, they speak, sing, and live their daily lives with praise and gratitude in the name of the Lord Jesus Christ (v. 20). This summarizes the essence of a believer worshiping God throughout each day of work and responsibility, within the community of faith, and as a witness to a world lost in darkness.

REFLECT Consider what it means to "follow God's example."

FRANK MOORE

SUBMISSION IN THE POWER OF THE SPIRIT

Healthy relationships among Christians include loving submission and sacrifice.

THE WORD

EPHESIANS 5:21-28

KEY VERSE

Submit to one another out of reverence for Christ. [22]Wives, submit yourselves to your own husbands as you do to the Lord. [23]For the husband is the head of the wife as Christ is the head of the church, his body, of which he is the Savior. [24]Now as the church submits to Christ, so also wives should submit to their husbands in everything.

[25]Husbands, love your wives, just as Christ loved the church and gave himself up for her [26]to make her holy, cleansing her by the washing with water through the word, [27]and to present her to himself as a radiant church, without stain or wrinkle or any other blemish, but holy and blameless. [28]In this same way, husbands ought to love their wives as their own bodies. He who loves his wife loves himself.

EPHESIANS 6:1-9

[1]Children, obey your parents in the Lord, for this is right. [2]"Honor your father and mother"—which is the first commandment with a promise—[3]"so that it may go well with you and that you may enjoy long life on the earth."

[4]Fathers, do not exasperate your children; instead, bring them up in the training and instruction of the Lord.

[5]Slaves, obey your earthly masters with respect and fear, and with sincerity of heart, just as you would obey Christ. [6]Obey them not only to win their favor when their eye is on you, but as slaves of Christ, doing the will of God from your heart. [7]Serve wholeheartedly, as if you were serving the Lord, not people, [8]because you know that the Lord will reward each one for whatever good they do, whether they are slave or free.

Unit 2: Ephesians

⁹And masters, treat your slaves in the same way. Do not threaten them, since you know that he who is both their Master and yours is in heaven, and there is no favoritism with him.

ENGAGE THE WORD

HUSBANDS AND WIVES

Ephesians 5:21-28

God instituted marriage when He created the first couple. Marriage remains, to this day, one of the cornerstones of civilization. Therefore, Christian believers must listen carefully to divine directives in order to apply biblical truths to their family relationships. This passage of Scripture has been one of the most misused and misunderstood passages in the Bible. Paul's message to husbands and wives is the opposite of what many readers think he intended.

Readers will understand the passage better by starting with the second half of verse 25. Paul used the metaphor of Christ as groom and His church as bride. Christ loved his bride so much that He offered himself as a selfless act in sacrificial death on the cross for her. He did this will two purposes in mind: "to make her holy" and to cleanse her (v. 26).

Why did Christ sacrifice himself for His bride? He wants to present her as radiant, dazzling, or beautiful. She glorifies God through the transforming work of the Holy Spirit in her life. Christ's sacrificial divine love makes her holy and blameless in word and deed. This glorious vision provides context for Paul's command: "Husbands love your wives just as Christ loved the church" (vv. 25, 28, 33). The verb in this phrase tells husbands to continually love their wives sacrificially, unconditionally, completely, and unselfishly. Husbands must seek the best interest of their wives and do anything to help them flourish.

Verses 22 and 24 refer back to the verb in the key verse for today (v. 21). This tells us that Paul commands both husbands and wives to mutually submit to one another out of reverence for Christ both in the church and home. This results in mutual love and a

CHILDREN AND PARENTS

SLAVES AND MASTERS

mutual partnership in marriage. Because "all believers should defer to one another in the life of the Christian community,"[1] the sacrificial love of Christ should guide the lives of His disciples in every setting.

Ephesians 6:1-4

As in the previous section, the first phrase of this passage refers back to the key verse regarding mutual submission to one another within the church (v. 21). Christian children must obey parental instructions. Paul stated the command with a slight variation in another epistle: "Children, obey your parents in everything, for this pleases the Lord" (Colossians 3:20).

Paul offers three reasons children should heed this command. First, every civilized culture in the world agrees that children do rightly by obeying their parents. Second, God's fifth commandment requires it. Third, the commandment also includes a divine provision; it promises that life goes better for those who respect and even care for their parents both while they live in the home and when parents reach old age.

Paul then offered counter-cultural instruction to fathers. Fathers must not lord it over their children and treat them any way they please. Proper discipline becomes necessary at times, but it must "never be excessive, unreasonable, abusive, arbitrary, unfair, constant, humiliating, or insensitive to the needs of children."[2] Proper discipline must include affirmation, training, and instruction in ways that draw children closer to the Lord. Their primary allegiance must always be to the Lord.

Ephesians 6:5-9

Roman rulers promoted the institution of slavery throughout the empire. All of the subservient nations that made up the Roman Empire maintained the status quo in order to demonstrate their allegiance to Rome. Paul's admonitions to slaves and masters did not imply that he agreed with Rome's institutional slavery.

Think About It

As a prisoner (3:1; 4:1; 6:20) of a totalitarian state, Paul simply could not have emancipated slaves. But by placing slaves and masters on equal footing before God, he sowed the seeds of slavery's eventual destruction (6:8). We cannot undo the sins of our ancestors. But, we can do something to end the scourges of racism and the new slavery of human-trafficking. And, we can practice zero-tolerance for domestic violence.

Society in this time period recognized slaves as members of the family, just like fathers, mothers, and children. The ancient Greco-Roman household structures Paul presumed no longer exist today. Paul's overarching command of the key verse for today, "Submit to one another out of reverence for Christ" (v. 21), affirmed that regardless of societal status within the body of Christ, we must have a mutual submission to one another because we serve the same God in heaven (v. 9). Paul's admonition to "serve wholeheartedly, as if you were serving the Lord" (v. 7) is similarly echoed in Colossians: "Whatever you do, work at it with all your heart, as working for the Lord, not for human masters" (Colossian 3:23). This command resonates with workers today in the way they regard their employers and the quality of the work they do for them.

As we read these verses, we must keep in mind that Christ breaks down all barriers and sounds the death knell of all abuse and misuse of humans. Christ, in His death, has placed everyone on level ground (see Galatians 3:28). Earthly status has no effect on His judgment. He rewards everyone fairly, justly, and righteously. God shows no favoritism!

In summary, all members of the Christian home must live lives that exhibit a continual filling with the Holy Spirit. Further, they must humbly practice mutual submission to one another as they worship and live under the lordship of Christ.

1. *NBBC: Ephesians, Colossians, Philemon* (Kansas City: Beacon Hill Press of Kansas City, 2019), 191.
2. Ibid, 206.

REFLECT Pray, asking God to open the eyes of our hearts to see what relationships a world transformed by Christ require today.

FRANK MOORE

BE STRONG IN THE LORD

May 24

The armor of God keeps us strong in the Lord as we engage in spiritual battles.

THE WORD

EPHESIANS 6:10-20

Finally, be strong in the Lord and in his mighty power. [11]Put on the full armor of God, so that you can take your stand against the devil's schemes. [12]For our struggle is not against flesh and blood, but against the rulers, against the authorities, against the powers of this dark world and against the spiritual forces of evil in the heavenly realms.

KEY VERSE [13]**Therefore put on the full armor of God, so that when the day of evil comes, you may be able to stand your ground, and after you have done everything, to stand.** [14]Stand firm then, with the belt of truth buckled around your waist, with the breastplate of righteousness in place, [15]and with your feet fitted with the readiness that comes from the gospel of peace. [16]In addition to all this, take up the shield of faith, with which you can extinguish all the flaming arrows of the evil one. [17]Take the helmet of salvation and the sword of the Spirit, which is the word of God.

[18]And pray in the Spirit on all occasions with all kinds of prayers and requests. With this in mind, be alert and always keep on praying for all the Lord's people. [19]Pray also for me, that whenever I speak, words may be given me so that I will fearlessly make known the mystery of the gospel, [20]for which I am an ambassador in chains. Pray that I may declare it fearlessly, as I should.

ENGAGE THE WORD

PREPARE FOR BATTLE

Ephesians 6:10-13

Paul uses the language of a military recruiter calling volunteers to enlist in God's army and gear up for battle. First, Paul says recruits must "be strong in the Lord" (v. 10) and continually lean into God's mighty power. Second, Paul says recruits must clothe themselves with the battle armor God provides for them. God's "full armor" gives them everything they need to defend themselves against enemies faced in spiritual warfare and to offensively go into battle when the Spirit leads the charge.

Paul challenges God's recruits to take their stand in the battles that lie ahead. That is, they must stand their ground, push back against the enemy, and live with a resolve against retreat. God does not expect believers to fight this battle alone. Paul is giving this battle cry to the entire community of faith which must work together to assure victory.

Believers battle against the devil's schemes in a variety of ways. Although not every negative situation or circumstance in life comes from Satan, the forces of evil are real; they come from the spiritual realm to oppose believers with the purpose of destroying their relationship with God. Believers who wear the full armor of God stand together in formation with other believers, and depend completely on Him for the divine power needed to resist Satan. They have God's assurance that they will still be standing strong when the dust of the battle settles.

THE ARMOR OF GOD

Ephesians 6:14-17

The full armor of God consists of seven items required for battle. Paul names six items in this section of material and one in the following section. While God graciously provides recruits with each of these items, individuals must take the responsibility of putting them on, learning to use them, and feeling comfortable enough when suited up in them to successfully fight in battle. Paul names the items God provides:

- *The belt of truth.* Believers fight not with the muscular strength of a bodybuilder, but with the authority that comes from having the reputation of being a person of integrity and always telling the truth. Truth here refers to the opposite of lying—speaking the orthodoxy of the gospel message.
- *The breastplate of righteousness.* Like a modern-day police officer's bullet-proof vest, God's recruits cover their chests with righteousness. Friends and family members know that these believers always seek to make wise ethical decisions, do the right thing whether it benefits them or not, live with integrity, and obey God's commands to the best of their ability.
- *Footwear of peace.* Antisemitism had opposed the Hebrew people for so many centuries that they did not define peace as the absence of war. Rather, peace to them meant the sense of well-being and victory that comes with God's salvation.
- *The shield of faith.* This piece of armor provides protection by living faithfully for God and trusting in Him for deliverance. They believe and live Hebrews 11:1: "Now faith is confidence in what we hope for and assurance about what we do not see." They trust the divine promise: "Never will I leave you; never will I forsake you" (Hebrews 13:5).
- *The helmet of salvation.* God protects recruit's heads with His salvation. New creatures in Christ live each day in the new identity Christ gives them. God's redemptive salvation protects them from the enemy's attack.
- *The sword of the Spirit.* All previous battle items have been defensive. This one can be used both for self-defense and offensive battle. This "is the only weapon Paul explained: which is the *proclaimed* word of God."[1] We need the Spirit to prevail, and God gives us His Word (Hebrews 4:12)

and the words to say (see Isaiah 49:2; Mark 13:11; Luke 12:11-12).

Ephesians 6:18-20

Paul presented here the seventh battle item—prayer. Spirit-inspired prayer is the most essential item in the entire list of equipment for victory over the forces of the evil one. Two instructions come with this call to prayer: be alert and be consistent. Diligent soldiers remain on high alert and constant guard when on duty. God's recruits must do the same. Well-rounded prayers include worship, praise, thanksgiving, confession, requests, intercession for the needs of others, and quiet listening. Not only must recruits remain on constant guard, they must live in a constant attitude of prayer. Effective prayer follows the guidance of the Holy Spirit, who leads seeking hearts to discern the will of God. We do not pray in an attempt to change God's mind; we pray to align ourselves with God's will.

Paul requested prayer from his readers. He did not ask them to pray for more creature comforts while in prison or to be released from bondage. Rather, he asked them seek the Spirit's leadership "that whenever I speak, words may be given me so that I will fearlessly make known the mystery of the gospel" (v. 19). His mission in life was to clearly proclaim the gospel message of Jesus Christ. Paul identified himself as an ambassador for Christ. In other words, He represented Jesus in this world. May the life goal of every disciple of Christ be to live and declare the gospel message.

1. *NBBC: Ephesians, Colossians, Philemon* (Kansas City: Beacon Hill Press of Kansas City, 2019) 221.

Think About It

"The crucifixion and resurrection of Jesus disarmed the hostile spiritual powers. Paul invited Christ's followers to join in the conflict, engaging the forces of evil armed only with the power of their God-given Christian virtues and prayer" (*NBBC: Ephesians, Colossians, Philemon* [Kansas City: Beacon Hill Press of Kansas City, 2019], 212).

THE MOST ESSENTIAL WEAPON

REFLECT Consider the ways you are incorporating the armor of God into your spiritual life.

FRANK MOORE

CONTENDING FOR THE FAITH

God has given us the responsibility of contending for the faith.

THE WORD

JUDE 1:3-8

Dear friends, although I was very eager to write to you about the salvation we share, I felt compelled to write and urge you to contend for the faith that was once for all entrusted to God's holy people. ⁴For certain individuals whose condemnation was written about long ago have secretly slipped in among you. They are ungodly people, who pervert the grace of our God into a license for immorality and deny Jesus Christ our only Sovereign and Lord.

⁵Though you already know all this, I want to remind you that the Lord at one time delivered his people out of Egypt, but later destroyed those who did not believe. ⁶And the angels who did not keep their positions of authority but abandoned their proper dwelling—these he has kept in darkness, bound with everlasting chains for judgment on the great Day. ⁷In a similar way, Sodom and Gomorrah and the surrounding towns gave themselves up to sexual immorality and perversion. They serve as an example of those who suffer the punishment of eternal fire.

⁸In the very same way, on the strength of their dreams these ungodly people pollute their own bodies, reject authority and heap abuse on celestial beings.

17-25

¹⁷But, dear friends, remember what the apostles of our Lord Jesus Christ foretold. ¹⁸They said to you, "In the last times there will be scoffers who will follow their own ungodly desires." ¹⁹These are the people who divide you, who follow mere natural instincts and do not have the Spirit.

KEY VERSES   ²⁰**But you, dear friends, by building yourselves up in your**

most holy faith and praying in the Holy Spirit, ²¹keep yourselves in God's love as you wait for the mercy of our Lord Jesus Christ to bring you to eternal life.

²²Be merciful to those who doubt; ²³save others by snatching them from the fire; to others show mercy, mixed with fear—hating even the clothing stained by corrupted flesh.

²⁴To him who is able to keep you from stumbling and to present you before his glorious presence without fault and with great joy—²⁵to the only God our Savior be glory, majesty, power and authority, through Jesus Christ our Lord, before all ages, now and forevermore! Amen.

ENGAGE THE WORD

CONTENDING FOR THE FAITH

Jude 1:3-8

After his greeting, Jude says that he originally intended the focus of this letter to be "the salvation we share." However, the news of certain false teachers among the people has led him to contend, or fight, for the faith. To speak of our shared faith, the church must be aware of what is false and careful to hold to the truth.

Specifically for Jude's original audience, there are people who seemingly believe in God but live like there isn't one. They exchange the grace of God for a kind of lawlessness, mistaking the good news of freedom in Christ as a license to do whatever they would like and to live as their own ruler. In doing so, they have rejected the only "Master and Lord," Jesus Christ.

That there are such "intruders" who oppose/reject the truth of God should not entirely come as a surprise to these believers. However, Jude reminds them of poignant examples from Scripture. The first is from Exodus. God saved the people from slavery; yet, due to their later disobedience, these chosen people were not immune from judgment. This is a warning for Christians that our belief in God should lead to a sustained and active faith.

The second example is that of angels who suc-

Jude talks about the fallen angels in 1:6. Though Jude's reference seems to focus on heavenly angelic beings, the Greek word for angel can also be translated as "messenger." So, this is an especially important image for what the church faces with false teachers. Just because one claims to be a messenger of God does not mean that their message comes from a heavenly place.

CAREFUL DISCERNMENT OF THE BELOVED

cumbed to pride and gave up their heavenly position (see Genesis 6:1-4; 2 Peter 2:4, 17). Jude contrasts the way that those who remain faithful to their calling are "kept for Jesus Christ," while the fate of these angels in darkness is judgment.

The final example is that of Sodom and Gomorrah, places destroyed because the people "went after flesh," or their "perversion" (v. 7). The condemnation of these cities was not just due to sexual immorality, though that was an aspect. Ezekiel helps give deeper context to their destruction: "Now this was the sin of your sister Sodom: She and her daughters were arrogant, overfed and unconcerned; they did not help the poor and needy (Ezekiel 16:49)." This is a reminder that the call of God is toward righteousness in all aspects of life.

Jude equates the false teachers to those condemned in these biblical examples and names their delusions for what they are—dreams to wake up from, a fairy tale with no good end.

Jude 1:17-25

Jude turns to contrasting the false teachers with the church. False teachers are people who scoff at authority, create division, chase after godless desires, celebrate what is physical, are devoid of the Spirit, and will receive judgement. Jude emphatically charges the church, saying, "but you" are to live differently than these false teachers (v. 17). The beloved in God are not to be scoffers, but are to remember the words of the apostles and heed them. The apostles warned them about heresy and so they must live in careful discernment and in steadfast faithfulness. The truth of the apostles' teachings leads the church to respond to false teachers by building their faith, praying in the Spirit, keeping in the love of God, and looking forward to the mercy of Christ. That is to say, rather than settle for the division caused by the false teachers, they should build one another up (v. 20) on the foundation of the "most holy" faith that they share (1 Corinthians 3:9-17; Ephesians 2:20-22).

Remaining true to a righteous path requires careful discernment by the church. Just claiming to be spiritual does not make it so. Prayerfully testing the motivations and fruit of one's actions will reveal whether something is in the Spirit. In the same way, merely naming something as "against" the Spirit does not mean that it necessarily is so. Being grounded in the truth of the gospel of Christ means seeking after Christ and not merely relying on our own interpretations or desires. Jude urges the church to turn away from fleshly things through careful and prayerful discernment.

The church, who is dedicated to remaining in God's love, should reflect the outcome of their faith—the mercy of Christ. Though Jude does not hold back from naming these false teachers for what they are, he calls the church to have discerning mercy even for these heretic. Jude emphasizes the urgency of calling people to the truth by saying that Christians are to "snatch others from the fire." Mercy should extend from the church to those who have been led astray by heresy, and even to the heretics themselves.

Jude finishes the letter with a doxology that affirms the hope of our shared salvation and counteracts the claims of the challengers. He proclaims that it is God who is able and willing to keep us from falling and hold us on the right path. Contrary to the actions and claims of the false teachers, it is only God who is our Savior and He alone who is worthy to the ascribe glory, majesty, power, and authority.

REFLECT How would you summarize the message of Jude?

AUSTIN TROYER is the pastor of Tahlequah Church of the Nazarene. He is also an adjunct professor at Southern Nazarene University.

False Teachers

The Marks of False Teachers

During time of Jude, false teachers, then as now, did not come into Christian congregations with warning placards hanging around their necks. To the contrary, they must have impressed the people with their friendliness, sincerity, and theological erudition; otherwise, no one would have given them the time of day. It was precisely because of their winsome personalities and sensible ideas that they were able to draw believers into their net.

How do we recognize the wolf masquerading in sheep's clothing? Jude gives us some clear markers. *First,* they are "godless" (v. 4b). Though they may look great, possess scintillating personalities, and talk a good line, there is a shallowness, a superficiality about their talk of God that sends up red flags.

Second, false teachers turn the marvelous "grace of our God into a license for immorality" (v. 4c). Since we are saved by grace and not by works, they say, it doesn't really matter what we do. This line of rationalization has led many a believer to ruin.

Third, false teachers elevate themselves as final authorities, answerable to no one. Jude identifies them as "dreamers . . . [who] reject authority," and who "speak abusively against whatever they do not understand" (vv. 8, 10). These false teachers grounded their moral license in special revelations. In a church culture enamored by the "independent ministry," we need to be wary of charismatic leaders who keep their devotees spellbound with all sorts of dreams and visions, but who are accountable to no one.

Fourth, false teachers enrich themselves at the expense of their followers. "Woe to them," says Jude, for "they have rushed for profit into Balaam's error." They are "shepherds who feed only themselves" (vv. 11-12). Balaam, a Moabite prophet, agreed to curse the Israelites for a reward. Being repeatedly warned against it by God, who even spoke to him through his donkey, Balaam blessed Israel instead of cursing them, and thus forfeited the reward. Nevertheless, there was larceny in his heart, and Jewish tradition has it that he did find a way to collect the money after all. In the end, Balaam met with an unhappy fate, for when the Israelites took vengeance against the Midianites, "they also killed Balaam son of Beor with the sword" (Numbers 31:8). In many ways Balaam represents the believer, who on the one hand is sensitive to the voice of God, but who on the other hand is slowly eaten up by lust and greed.

God's Judgment upon False Teachers

What Jude gives us in his "wake-up call" letter is a long exposition of a short Pauline verse, "For the wages of sin is death" (Romans 6:23a). *First,* Jude reminds us of what happened to the rebellious and unbelieving generation of Israelites that came out of Egypt: they were all "destroyed" except for Joshua and Caleb (v. 5). Those who "pollute their own bodies" and "reject authority" (v. 8) will likewise be judged the same way by God.

Second, Jude refers to the sin of angels "who did not keep their positions of authority but abandoned their own home" (v. 6). This refers to the story in Genesis 6:1-5, where "the sons of God saw that the daughters of men were beautiful, and they married any of them they chose" (6:2). Not only were giants born to the women, but "every inclination of the thoughts of the human heart was only evil all the time" (6:5). This produced a race of people so corrupt that God resolved to "wipe from the face of the earth the human race" (6:7). Those who commit immorality, and teach others to do the same, will suffer the same fate.

Third, Jude cites the well-known fiery destruction of Sodom and Gomorrah as a warning of what happened to those who "gave themselves up to sexual immorality and perversion." *Fourth,* Jude quotes Enoch's prophecy, found in the apocryphal First Book of Enoch, in which he warns Noah's generation of God's holy judgment upon "all the ungodly" and all their "ungodly acts," along with "all the harsh words ungodly sinners have spoken against [the Lord]" (Jude 1:15).

This portrait of God's judgment and destruction troubles some Christians. Jude, however, says, "these are the very things that destroy them" (v. 10b). This would be in accord with Paul's portrayal of God's wrath upon human godlessness and wickedness as "God gave them over" (Romans 1:24, 26, 28) to suffering the consequences of their own sin. It is God allowing the self-destructiveness intrinsic in sin to work itself out in the lives of those who reject the truth of God's Word and chose to live as they choose to live, rather than living God's way.

The Antidote to False Teachers

It is important to see that Jude does not fire up Christians to become full-time "heresy-hunters," nor does he incite them to conduct Inquisitions. Rather, he encourages them to keep their focus on Christ in several ways. *First,* he reminds them that they should not be surprised over the presence of "scoffers who will follow their own ungodly desires" (v. 18), because such attacks had been foretold by "the apostles of our Lord Jesus Christ" (v. 17). *Second,* Jude encourages them to build "yourselves up in your most holy faith and pray in the Holy Spirit" (v. 20).

Third, Jude counsels believers to "keep yourselves in God's love as you wait for the mercy of our Lord Jesus Christ to bring you to eternal life" (v. 21). We must remember that nobody has a greater interest in bringing us to eternal life than God. We can rest in the confidence that He is always at work in us by "the Holy Spirit" to do everything necessary, without compromising our freedom, to bring us into eternal salvation. "If God be for us," asks Paul, "who can be against us?" (Romans 8:31).

Fourth, Jude urges the church not to be harsh and judgmental toward those who have been drawn into the web of false teaching, but rather "Be merciful to those who doubt; save others by snatching them from the fire; to others show mercy, mixed with fear—hating even the clothing stained by corrupted flesh" (vv. 22-23). This is a cautionary word for those whose first response to real or perceived heretics is to demonize them and drive them from the church. If we lovingly and carefully reach out to them in mercy rather than contempt, there is always the possibility that their eyes will be opened and that they will repent and embrace the gospel.

Finally, Jude concludes with one of the most eloquent doxologies—an offering of praise that affirms God's power to keep us "from falling and to present [us] before his glorious presence without fault and with great joy" (v. 24). When we resist false teaching and turn our eyes toward Jesus, we, too, will ascribe glory, majesty, power and authority to "the only God our Savior . . . Jesus Christ our Lord . . . now and forevermore! Amen" (v. 25).

Getting the Most Out of Your Prayer Time

"Do not be anxious about anything, but in every situation, by prayer and petition, with thanksgiving, present your requests to God. And the peace of God, which transcends all understanding, will guard your hearts and your minds in Christ Jesus" (Philippians 4:6-7).

Plan: We all live busy lives. Finding time for personal prayer in the morning and/or evening can be difficult. Look for times such as before breakfast, during lunchtime, or just before bedtime. Whatever time you choose, be sure to make it a regular part of your daily life.

Perspective: Foster a "want to" rather than a "have to" experience. Consider incorporating Scripture, singing, and time to pray for others.

Patience: Don't be in a hurry. Take time to pray (speaking to God), but also allow time for silence (listening to God speak through His presence and Word).

Purpose: The goal is not to "do" prayer, but to grow closer to God.

Participation: Consider, if possible, a time for family/small group prayer. Invite various members to read, pray, and so on. Create an atmosphere of participation.

[Adapted from *Wesley Prayers for Families: A Paraphrase* (Kansas City: The Foundry Publishing, 2020.]

Key Verse Memory

Committing God's Word to memory is an important goal for Christians of every age. To assist you in this worthy objective, we have suggested three key verses for memorization. Select one verse to memorize each month or memorize one verse of your choosing for the quarter.

Key verses for Spring 2026:

Philippians 1:21

Philippians 3:13-14

Ephesians 5:1

COMING NEXT QUARTER

Summer 2026

Unit 1: Hard Sayings of the New Testament

Have you ever wondered what Jesus meant when He said, "If anyone . . . does not hate father and mother, wife and children, brothers and sisters . . . such a person cannot be my disciple" (Luke 14:26)? During this study, we will explore some of the harder sayings of the New Testament.

Unit 2: A Charge to Keep (1 Timothy)

Timothy was one of the apostle Pauls closest colleagues. During his third missionary journey, Paul charged Timothy with the care of the church at Ephesus. In this unit, we will examine Paul's first letter to Timothy and discover how this first-century letter was written to us as well.